THE

JAGUAR

SARAH HOLLAND-BATT

UQP

First published 2022 by University of Queensland Press
PO Box 6042, St Lucia, Queensland 4067 Australia
Reprinted 2022 (twice), 2023 (twice)

University of Queensland Press (UQP) acknowledges the Traditional Owners
and their custodianship of the lands on which UQP operates. We pay our respects
to their Ancestors and their descendants, who continue cultural and spiritual
connections to Country. We recognise their valuable contributions to Australian
and global society.

uqp.com.au
reception@uqp.com.au

Cover design by Josh Durham (Design by Committee)
Cover photograph by Staffan Widstrand
Typeset in 11.5/14 pt Adobe Garamond Pro by Post Pre-press Group, Brisbane
Printed in Australia by McPherson's Printing Group

 **Queensland Government** University of Queensland Press is supported by the
Queensland Government through Arts Queensland.

 Australian Government **Australia Council for the Arts** University of Queensland Press is
assisted by the Australian Government
through the Australia Council, its arts
funding and advisory body.

A catalogue record for this book is available from the National Library of Australia.

ISBN 978 0 7022 6550 1 (pbk)
ISBN 978 0 7022 6671 3 (epdf)
ISBN 978 0 7022 6762 8 (epub)

University of Queensland Press uses papers that are natural, renewable and
recyclable products made from wood grown in well-managed forests and other
controlled sources. The logging and manufacturing processes conform to the
environmental regulations of the country of origin.

MIX
Paper | Supporting
responsible forestry
FSC
www.fsc.org   FSC® C001695

Sarah Holland-Batt is an award-winning poet, editor and critic, and Professor of Creative Writing and Literary Studies at QUT. Her first book, *Aria* (UQP, 2008), received numerous literary awards, and her second book, *The Hazards* (UQP, 2015), won the Prime Minister's Literary Award for Poetry in 2016. Her most recent book is *Fishing for Lightning* (UQP, 2021), a collection of her poetry columns written for *The Australian*. She is the recipient of a Sidney Myer Creative Fellowship, the W.G. Walker Memorial Fulbright Scholarship, residencies at Yaddo and MacDowell in the United States, the Marten Bequest Scholarship, an Asialink Literature Residency in Japan, and an Australia Council Literature Residency at the B.R. Whiting Studio in Rome, among other honours. She is presently the Judy Harris Writer in Residence at the Charles Perkins Centre at The University of Sydney.

Also by Sarah Holland-Batt

Poetry
Aria
The Hazards

As editor
The Best Australian Poems 2016
The Best Australian Poems 2017

Essays
Fishing for Lightning: The spark of poetry

for my father—
Über Sternen muß er wohnen

CONTENTS

I

II

III

IV

yet to sing love,
love must first shatter us

—H.D.

I

My Father as a Giant Koi

My father is at the bottom of a pond
perfecting the art of the circle.
He is guiding the mottled zeppelin
of his body in a single unceasing turn
like a monorail running on greased steel,
like an ice skater swerving on a blade.
His scales are lava and ember dappled with carbon.
His tail, a luxurious Japanese fan.
He is so far beneath the green skin of duckweed
he cannot make me out, or I him.
What he knows is shrinking into round facts:
days like mossed stones, each the same weight,
spears of water hyacinth rising
around him like jail bars, reek of peat.
He has been down there for years—
ancient god of the dark, keeper of the single
koan, moving in currents only he can sense,
fluent as a windsock. He surfaces
three times a day when the nurse brings
a tray—cold blanched carrot and beef,
whitesauce fillet of whiting, pound cake.
He cannot trust the scratched headlamps
of his eyes so he navigates by feel,
angling his huge whiskered head
mouth-first towards the fork, weaving
like an adder charmed by smoke,
then he bites down to find the world
suddenly there again, solid as metal and bait.

The Gift

In the garden, my father sits in his wheelchair
garlanded by summer hibiscus
like a saint in a seventeenth-century cartouche.
A flowering wreath buzzes around his head—
passionate red. He holds the gift of death
in his lap: small, oblong, wrapped in black.
He has been waiting seventeen years to open it
and is impatient. When I ask how he is
my father cries. His crying comes as a visitation,
the body squeezing tears from his ducts tenderly
as a nurse measuring drops of calamine
from an amber bottle, as a teen at the carwash
wringing a chamois of suds. It is a kind of miracle
to see my father weeping this freely, weeping
for what is owed him. *How are you?* I ask again
because his answer depends on an instant's microclimate,
his moods bloom and retreat like an anemone
as the cold currents whirl around him—
crying one minute, sedate the next.
But today my father is disconsolate.
I'm having a bad day, he says, and tries again.
I'm having a bad year. I'm having a bad decade.
I hate myself for noticing his poetry—the triplet
that should not be beautiful to my ear
but is. Day, year, decade—scale of awful economy.
I want to give him his present but it is not mine
to give. We sit as if mother and son on Christmas Eve
waiting for midnight to tick over, anticipating
the moment we can open his present together—

first my father holding it up to his ear and shaking it,
then me helping him peel back the paper,
the weight of his death knocking,
and once the box is unwrapped it will be mine,
I will carry the gift of his death endlessly,
every day I will know it opening in me.

The Parachute

All night my father hangs upside down
in the hospital basement
trapped under the giant pulsing bell
of a crystal jellyfish. He is buckled in—
snaps of metal crisscross his thorax, a tangle
of suspension lines skein around his legs.
Ripstop nylon billows and shrinks above him:
canopy of army green, a fever skin.
He cannot understand how he landed behind enemy lines
in this crawlspace, its jumble of copper pipes
and surplus gear. He moves slow as an insect in agar.
His eyes are blind and shine with effort.
His rig is snagged on some unseen obstacle—
a tree, or the intimation of a tree.
His fatigues he recognises, but the parachute
is his father's—the one that failed to deploy
when his Hawker Hurricane was shot down
over France. He is in for observation,
or is it reconnaissance—the mission keeps moving—
but there's a keyhole in the fabric above his head:
a clear pupil, the apex vent, portal
to a world he might see through to
if only he could reach it, if only he wasn't
plummeting further with every breath.

Brazil

My mother and I eat take-out: crispy basil prawn and red duck curry. Last week in his nursing home, my father told my mother he was taking her to Brazil. He'd been thinking about where to go for a long time, he said, and landed on Brazil. Its borders touch ten countries, he said, which is convenient. How long are we going for? my mother asked. At least a year, he said. Will we see the Amazon? my mother asked. Oh yes. And Sarah? my mother asked. She'll have to come, my father said. I don't know if she can, my mother said, she has to work. Her work will understand, my father said. I taste lychee and chilli. My mother sips her wine. We're going first-class, my father said. We've been married for fifty years, and you deserve it. My mother spoons curry over coconut rice as she tells me this. The rice is rich and sweet. I just thanked him, she said. I knew he'd forget all about it. But my father didn't forget. The next day, he said he'd been running the numbers, and he wasn't sure whether he could afford to go to Brazil first-class, but we would definitely go business. And I see it, I see my father at 40,000 feet, I see him craning his neck to look out of the window, I see him flying over Mato Grosso do Sul, I see him flying like a distant god over cerrado savannah and the snaking wetlands of the Pantanal, I see my father touching the corner of his mouth with a linen napkin as the plane begins its descent, its wings flexing, I see the silverware gleaming in front of him, I see him lifting a cup filled with jaguar's blood up to the light, how it gleams like wine, I see the raw jaguar's heart filleted in the finest slivers, carmine red, laid out like a stinking meat flower in front of him.

Empires of Mind

Beside the fountain's troupe of sun-bleached rubber ducks,
in the gardens, under a shade sail,
my father is crying about Winston Churchill.
Midway through a lunch of cremated schnitzel
spoonfed by the carer with the port-wine stain
my father is crying about Winston Churchill.

In the night he cries out for Winston Churchill.
During his morning bath he cries for Winston Churchill.
When the nurse does up his buttons, he will not stop his weeping.
When the therapist wheels him to Tuesday piano
my father ignores the Mozart and cries for Winston Churchill.

He cries not like a child seeking absolution,
not like the mourner or the mourned, but free and unconstrained
as one who has spent a long time denying an urge
and is suddenly giddy and incontinent in his liberation.

The cleaners are unmoved. The woman
who brings his hourly cup of pills is bright as a firework
and goes about her round with the hardness
of one who has heard all the crying in the world
and finds in that reservoir nothing more disturbing
than a tap's dripping drumbeat in a sink.

But the night supervisor is frightened
in the early hours when the halls ping
with the sharp beep of motion sensors and my father's crying.

His longing for silence is fierce and keen
as a pregnant woman's craving for salt and fried chicken,
as my father's crying for Winston Churchill.

And the women in their beds call for it to stop like a Greek chorus
croaking like bullfrogs each to each in the dark—
unsettled, loud, insatiable—the unutterable fear
rippling through them like a herd of horses
apprehending the tremor of thunder
on a horizon they cannot see but feel.

The Gurney

Because the gurney is unattended
in the hallway outside my father's room,
because nobody is guarding its bright metal rails
or its silver tongue shrouded with a woollen blanket,
because the blanket is a faded shade
of redcurrant—now bitter, now sweet—
because the hallway is empty
of everything but soothing lemon wallpaper
and the eucalypt sting of disinfectant,
I am almost beside it before I see
the unmistakable topography of a body—
troughs and peaks, a rough silhouette
as though earth is piled up there, underneath.
The hairs on my arms rise stiffly
like the prickling pelt of a nettle leaf,
and as if I have suddenly held copper
wire to current I am seized
with an uncontrollable shudder
summoned from some primordial place
behind the daylight mind. Mortal voice, speak.
Don't move, I want to say, *I'll get somebody*—
but I do not know to whom I am speaking,
I do not know whose body I will raise,
there is no helping what is beyond
help, no speaking to what is beyond
speech. My father's voice pipes from his room—
a rising inflection that means he is arguing
with the nurse about his medication—
and I am woozy, ecstatic: this body is not

his, he is still wrapped in his voice, if I shook him
he would rattle with it, it would spear
from him like a germinating seed,
the green pellet of it spiking open,
rolling his life out on gimballing wheels.

Time Remaining

Like rolled beads of mercury
silver bubbles fly up silently
in the mineral water by my father's bed.

A bag of Hartmann's Solution
hangs in the air like a sling
of trapped rain.

A chartreuse teardrop
blinks on the infusion pump's screen.
The gauge reads *Time Remaining.*

In this void of time
in which my father remains—
I want to say, *is remaining*—

present continuous—he returns to me.
Hello sweetheart, he says blurrily.
I'm just trying to get the damned thing working.

And as if I can see what he's seeing
I ask, *Is it plugged in?*
He says, *I'm beginning to wonder*

and he's gone again, eyes swivelling
through the morphine, rolling
in the mulberry velvet of it

and I can see it's true: my father is beginning
to wonder, he is at the verge
of something he is only starting

to comprehend the shape of
as if he's standing at the delta
of a huge muddy rivermouth

where the mackerel-backed sky and water
mirror each other's enormities
and the eye cannot find the horizon

between them—a demarcation known only
to those who wade in, full immersion.
It is right that at the end of his life

my father's final feeling is wonder—
not awe, not joy, but wonder—
cousin of astonishment and doubt,

which in the Old English
also means to magnify—
the way his time remaining

dilates and shrinks, is made
both infinitesimally small and infinite:
a day, an hour, a minute.

Lime Jelly

Your last burning day
you were thirsty

but couldn't drink.
Even thickened water

jerked in the throat.
Your chest churned

with hot asphalt,
slurry of phlegm,

a rumble
of distant thunder.

The flannels
I dipped in cold

scorched
your forehead.

Nurses swabbed your mouth
with sponge lollipops—

minted disinfectant
to mask death's stink.

Grace came as a nurse
who thought of jelly—

a single fluted cup,
electric green, spooned

wibbling to your lips.
Its slick sugars

bypassed swallowing.
You managed

the whole tubful—
a last rite so tender

months later
it leaves me trembling.

The Kindest Thing

The doctor with an Armani model's jawline
is brisk when he tells me the kindest thing
is to withhold antibiotics.
Pneumonia is the old man's friend, he says,
his stare so piercing I feel compelled
by his beauty—he is almost shining
with charisma and vitality, this man who coaxes
patients towards death like an emerald boa
stretching its pink jaw by inches
until the glass frog is entirely inside the snake's head,
subsumed into the hypnotic knot of its body,
its scales flexing electric green as new leaves,
its white lightning bolts rippling and contracting—
or like the sinister musk blossoming
of an orchid mantis—limbs variegated
like borlotti beans in flecked rose and cream—
swaying like a silken flower to lure
the dreaming crickets in. The kindest thing
is to hand yourself up to death's calling,
I know this, but I am not handing myself up,
I am offering over my father, tenderly
unhinging death's jaws until he is swamped
with fever, his pupils tracking some invisible thread
as he eases into unconsciousness, his eyes
bright with the knowledge of one
who senses he is being carried away
but does not know why or where.

Terminal Lucidity

After twenty years away, an intercession of clarity
in your final hours: surfacing from a morphine surge,
suddenly you were there again,
your eyes lighting on my face, gold-panned hazel,
alive with the old intelligence.
In the small hospital room at the corridor's end
we listened to Clair de Lune
as vague rain prickled outside in the garden bed.
You listened, dozed, awoke. I spoke,
and you stayed until my words petered out,
then stayed through the silence after.
It's all silence now—the profound silence
which makes all other silences loud—
yet in the caesurae of days, I hear you listening.

Nessun Dorma

When I first see my father's body
it is just after midnight, his face bathed
in mute fluorescence, a stark white sheet
pulled tight to his neck—and I remember
how towards the end of his life
all my father wanted was to watch Pavarotti,
his face lilac in the laptop's moonlight,
looping a concert in LA in 1994 over and over.
First the uneasy chorus whispering *nessun dorma*,
nessun dorma, then the bright strings entering,
il principe ignoto Calaf—brows livid,
hair corkscrewing with sweat, eyes brown
as a hound's—opens his throat, hitting the alveolar trill
on *dorma* like a drumroll, thunder, leather, cognac,
tobacco, liquorice, anise, the dark richness surging,
his mouth's aperture not wide enough
for the sound rolling out, my father's head craning
like a sunflower to absorb its fullness,
the villagers sleepless under threat of execution,
hunting for a name by dawn, the night gardens bristling
with lilies, aster, moonflower, jasmine—
the camera panning in on Pavarotti's face,
his shoulders thick as concrete, unfeeling Turandot
up in her cold bedroom, stars like knife-tips
above her, and Calaf burning with his secret,
ma il mio mistero è chiuso in me, Pavarotti singing
from under his brow now, his chin tucked
like a diver's, only his eyebrows like accents,
tenuto, marcato, moving, the chorus light as mist

drifting in—we must die, we must die—
the well of Pavarotti's mouth deepening,
his head tugged back by the force
of his voice—crucible of virgin metal,
burning pour—*tramontate, stelle,*
and after he reaches the climactic fourth octave,
the heroic B and the sustained A,
he lets his head loll back and closes his eyes,
mouth agape and ecstatic, as my father's mouth
was open when he died, knowing the performance
was over, waiting for the faint rain of applause.

The Outing

You kept your clothing divided
into *round the house* and *going out*.

After you could do neither
your wardrobe still upheld your order,

a museum piece
preserving old exigencies—

wool Pierre Cardin suits to the left,
grey trackpants to the right.

Before you died, the mortician
asked for an outfit

for your cremation. In their right place
I found your best navy slacks

furzed with mildew—
so long since their last outing.

I washed them—how
could I not—held them

hot to my cheek—ghosting
of chamomile detergent—

pressed them crisp
with your favourite

gingham shirt, still sharp
after twenty years. I know

you'd insist they be just so,
faultless. After a week

broiling in your own skin
sliding delirious in a paper gown

under artic air-conditioning,
in the end you'll be dressed

as a man again—someone
with somewhere, finally, to go.

The Clearing

In a dark wood I find it again—
chrome luge, weathered rails.
Its wheels are sunk in clay.
It has lain a long time in the mind.
Strangled by wildflower and weed
it is no longer the thing itself but the idea of the thing:
not a gurney but grassblade and surge,
greengage roped with blossom,
streak of angelica, afterburn of aster.
It blew here one green evening—
rattled brakeless over rock, veering sideways
like a spooked animal, juddering
down culvert and hill to the clearing.
Then rewilding began—
mock orange crabbing over steel
by inch and fist, haul and ache,
honeysuckle swallowing bullet nubs of rivets,
empire of trumpet flower furring the tongue.
In the undergrowth, a storm of milkweed
beaded with mercury,
wild iris skewered by nerves of rain.
What lies beneath is not the thing
but the memory of the thing—
not the gurney
but the shape of a gurney,
not my father
but the shadow of his body,
groundcover fed by needleprick and wire of blood,
veins of sap and woodring, blossom

of his breath, vine and wreath, the red
holly and the white pine, ghost
of his hair and teeth in the moon's hangnail,
feral mouse's tail, the fir and the sable, sturdiness
of the world, moss and skullcap, rat stink
and badger reek, perfume and decay—
and underfoot, hulls of dead leaves
dry as the boats that floated a pharaoh's body
down the waterless river
freighted with beer and barley—
fuel for a sky burial, waterlily blue—
vision of a single grain
trembling on its stem, then gone again.

At Springbrook

All day rainbows have burnt
and faltered on the retina
as showers blow through the valley
disorienting ancient eucalypts
on the edge of the gorge,
their branches lashing like kelp
in a squall. Now and then a limb
falls on the roof. Between gusts
it's quiet. The valley's ridges
are leached by mist, distinguishable
only as perforated lines in smoke blue.
The cockatoos who sharpened their way
through the air at dawn are gone.
I carry in heartwood for the stove.
When I swing open its glass door
a greying bee falls from the grate.
Tufted with ash, it moves ponderously
as though each of its legs is trying
to tune an instrument independently—
plucking the strings, sounding the notes.
The bee is not long for this world—
my father's phrase. He said it about anything
losing its function—a lawnmower,
a kettle, a lamp—all not long for this world.
The bee curls on its side. In the end
my father was both not long
and too long for this world.
I scoop the bee in a barque of newspaper
and ferry it onto the grass.

It latches to a green spear, and stops.
These days I forget intermittently
that my father is dead—
for hours, sometimes, he lives again.
Soon, I tell you, everything
will be washed by rain.

II

Thalassography

I have known these estuaries—
the channels and canals, the backwaters
that flush and eddy to the Pacific,

I have skimmed that muddied slurry,
felt the nip in the throat
where the salt in the air is the salt of the coast,

I have tacked where the tide is incomplete:
no rollers and breakers,
only an ebb that rocks the wayfarers—

a rush of silver, the gavel-smack of mullet
in the night, mud crabs elbowing
denwards under concrete slabs of boat ramps—

I have stalked where herons stilt and spear
baitfish in green afternoons,
cast crab pots in loose analemmas

to watch the black sonar spread,
tracked prawn trawlers on the broadwater
crawling back in the lavender dawn

then sat at the jetty's edge
and shucked those tiger shells,
cast sucked heads back into the dark,

crushed mussels underfoot
for the burn of sharpened chitin,
stepped where stingrays wallow and idle,

shuffling their barbs, waiting to strike.
I have spent half my life in low tide—
nights where I have not known

if I am contracting or dragging out again,
where the movement of the water
is the movement of my mind—

unending comings and goings
of sounds and narrows, those entry points
to my two continents—and my history

is the history of currents: a canal small enough
to catch a childhood in its net,
water vast enough to divide a life.

Light Years

All summer the northern flickers
hammered our conservatory,
pitting the cedar cladding

with inconsolable ovals.
They let the wind in.
Battered, the house flexed.

My father climbed a ladder,
meshed the eaves. No difference.
Nothing could stop them.

From the upstairs window seat
I could see the volcanic surge
of their red cheeks working, working.

I knew how it felt to want
to drill to the centre of the earth,
tunnel to the Old World.

All summer I sent letters
to a continent so distant
it made me think of physics—

the Pacific spread out,
its impossible witness
like light years, a curvature

I could not measure.
I knew I was farther away
than time, that when I re-entered

my hemisphere
I would be changed,
estranged by all that moondust.

Outdoors, the birds nail-gunned on.
The damage spread.
By fall, my accent shifted.

Mountain vowels crept in,
nouns curled in my mouth.
Finally, we called a man

who set traps, mounted
a false hawk on the roof.
The day the hawk came

I watched the flickers hover in terror
then shear away, nerves shot.
Then it was winter: snow loomed,

and they flew south for good.
I waited to feel the change.
Everywhere the dark holes grew.

Pikes Peak

Hiking near the timberline at twelve thousand feet
my father mistakes an almost silent stroke for vertigo—
immobilisation that arrives like a tsunami,
the body withdrawing to its furthest reaches,
brain stem stoppered for a paralysing second.
He sits winded in a rubble of rose granite
staring at the infinite regression of quaking aspen,
valley after valley to the horizon,
stunned by his own elevation. Then fear,
comprehension: he has lost the language
for water, aspirin. An icy breeze shearing
off snow, heads of spruce and bristlecone
stretching all the way down to the switchback
roads where motorcycles lean in terminal arcs.
At this height everything grows deformed
by wind and cold—flag trees with a single comb
of greenery down a leeward side,
krummholz pines twisted into pretzel bends,
scratchings of alpine parsley, dwarf clover.
Who knows exactly when it started or was over—
a lightning storm in the skull, its barometer
registering no drop in pressure—then whole zones
denuded like the palms after Castle Bravo—
detonation raising storeys of ocean to the sky.
I gave myself a fright, he says, and shakes his head—
a bull shifting a cloud of horseflies.
Around my father tundra grass is blowing
grain by stunted grain. This is the vista
about which Katharine Lee Bates wrote *America*

the Beautiful—the only line of which I ever remember
is *O beautiful for pilgrim feet*, which to me
means precisely zero. But if I strain I can still see him
sitting dumbfounded in that field of feldspar,
his beautiful pilgrim feet laced into white Reeboks and gym socks
as a sunburst ripples through his brain.
My father is calm as a monk whose long meditation
produces imperceptible shifts
in his physiognomy, and I understand
he went up the mountain for the same reason
everyone goes up mountains.
He went up the mountain to change.

Substantia Nigra

A cross-section of my father's brain
flares on the hospital lightbox
like a shaving of white truffle,
a botanical specimen licked with radium.
What should be the mind's blackest region
fluoresces white, tinged with violet.

The neurologist explains my father's vanishing
substantia nigra—Latin for *black substance*,
midnight bullet of memory.
Bleaching the size of a broadbean
is turning my father jerky, compulsive.

My mind drifts to intelligence gathering—
carbon coating of Nighthawks and drones,
dazzle camouflage, Vantablack bending
light inwards. Even the black ops of animals
depend on darkness—bats' ultrasound
pinging off sunless caves, sugar gliders
paratrooping through velvet.

My father doesn't miss the darkness.
He takes the news calm as a stone.
I want to slap him. He of all people knows
the worst thing in science fiction
is exactly this failure—the craft in deep space
whose stealth defences crash
in a craze of sirens, the worst
scudding towards it like an asteroid
and the captain suddenly naked in the light again.

The Midpoint

Here heat is the only constancy.
The coast road dips
into troughs of liquid mercury,
rounds its way
to the headland's crest,
tails to tufted dunes
where a troupe of kelp gulls
fossick in spinifex.
At the water's edge
three sandpipers
print the just-wet sand
like setting cement,
a single-file funeral procession
stepping to the rockpool.
No blue sloops knifing
the breakers today—
only a white-bellied sea eagle
grieving an endless loop,
cicadas soldering the air.
I am a creature of this
inhospitable place—
sun that desiccates,
migrainous light that binds—
the copper taipan knotting
around some soft body,
its jaws impossible
to prise from its desire,
the salt breeze harrying
magenta detonations

of pigface daisies,
the whelk surging
into its shell with the tide,
everything that clings
and clutches and hews.
I am midway through
whatever you could call
a life—my systole
and diastole seizing
at the root. No language
for this brute insistence.
Hellfire days. Strangling nights.
Still I want
what I want—
which is to endure.

Tijuana

My father is standing on the border
between self and other—seized by gremlin,
dybbuk, malevolent haunt. His mood-shifts
turn apocalyptic—the curses when they come
arrive as darts tipped with electric blue venom
so sharp it brings paralysis. *I am a bitch,*
I am a destroyer—so says the ventriloquist spirit
moving his jaw. Decades ago, over dinner
of mashed potato and overdone pork,
my father swore he would drive to Tijuana
and bribe a vet for vials of Nembutal. *I'll go out*
with cervezas and empanadas, he said,
I'll never become a vegetable. This I remember.
But my father was a liar. He took us
to Santa Fe instead—pointless pilgrimage
to the abandoned crutches and canes at Chimayó,
adobe church girt by ersatz healing dirt.
Now some other personality squats in him,
impossible to evict. In a bar in Mexico City
I pound shots of mezcal with lime chasers,
lay scalding wafers of habanero chilli
on my tongue. I lift the glass to the light,
toast my father—I am taking communion
with whatever burns. The bartender asks
no questions, stacks tumblers into crates
like he is racking pool balls, brings me more.
I want to tell him I am steeling myself to caustic tastes—
lemon rind, peppercorn, *mirto bianco,*
sting of tartest greens, sour chicory—

so when the time comes, I will hold my nerve,
I will drink the phenobarbital like holy water,
let it run like smoke down my throat
because I know there is no ending
more difficult than my father's, there is nothing
more bitter to swallow in this world.

Kneeling Figure

My mother keeps her patellas sealed
in an airmail envelope: hazelnut brown,
they have mummified here fifty years—
creaking nubbins that never worked
squealed like chalk in the joint
until a Harley Street surgeon plucked them out.

Then, a full-leg fibreglass cast
and permanent contraction:
no jogging or sitting cross-legged,
pinhole pain at each stair.

When friends came around
I drew the snug pucks out
like a magic trick—what was inside
is now out—and they'd scream, hysterical.

Like neglected pets, they've gone feral
in the envelope's dewy conservatory,
bone leathered into tallow apricot
glazed with an unidentifiable film.

I take one into my hand—a wax pat
the weight of a skimming stone.
Hinge of the body, pivot of grief—they would not bend
for her father's cancer or her mother's death,
they would not genuflect
for her husband's diagnosis or long descent—

but one day this dank envelope
will reach its destination,
like a scrolled and brined message
roiling half a century across the ocean
in a coffin of cataracted seaglass
before it lands on the beach of her

and my mother will wake fluent
in all the motions she has endlessly understudied,
and walk out into her garden
among the stiff orange flames
of birds-of-paradise and the unyielding spines
of water-holding aloes, and kneel.

The Jaguar

It shone like an insect in the driveway:
iridescent emerald, out-of-season Christmas beetle.
Metallic flecks in the paint like riverbed tailings,
squeaking doeskin seats. *Bottle green*, my father called it,
or else *forest*. A folly he bought without test-driving,
vintage 1980 XJ, a rebellion against his tremor.
The sole bidder, he won the auction without trying
the day after the doctor told him to draw a line
under his driving years. My mother didn't speak
for weeks. It gleamed on the terracotta drive,
wildcat forever lunging on the hood,
predatory, the chrome snagging in the sun,
ornament of my father's madness,
miraculous and sleek, until he started to tinker,
painted the leather seats with acrylic
so they peeled and cracked, jacked the gearstick,
hacked a hole into the dash with a Stanley knife,
jury-rigged the driver's seat so it sat so low
you couldn't see over the dash. For months
he drove it even though my mother begged,
he drove it as though he was punishing her,
dangerously fast on the back roads, then
opened up the engine on the highway, full
throttle, even though he was going blind in one eye,
even though my mother and I refused to get in,
and for the first time in years my father
was happy—he was happy to be driving,
he was happy my mother and I
were miserable. Finally his modifications

killed it, the car he always wanted and waited
so long to buy, and it sat like a carcass
in the garage, like a headstone, like a coffin—
but it's no symbol or metaphor. I can't make anything of it.

The Odds

Easiest to comprehend the odds
as a pair of hands with stiff white cuffs
shuffling three upturned cups
in the mesmeric loops of a spirograph
across an immaculate tablecloth.
It's a hustler's game of thimblerig, shell and pea
laid out just for me: my future
rattling under a metal dome—
the possibility up to one in three,
a do or dare, ride or die genetic lottery,
light as air, hard as fact. It's an act—
pretending I don't care. The percentages bend,
depend on things unseen: a kink in the genes,
armadillo repeats and alpha helices
crimped into hairpin arrangement,
the mutation called LRRK2, dardarin—
from the Basque for *trembling*—
that could send me one of three ways,
two in which I duck the curse, and a third
diagnosis served up with a flourish
in some melon green doctor's surgery—
doomed to repeat my father's long extinguishment,
the resting tremor, the rictus,
no match snuff, but years of this slow ossifying,
stretched out in front of me, utterly fucked.
Pick a hand, tap a cup—time's up.

The Grip

The mud crabs shadowboxed
when my father prised them from wicker—
lopsided nips that could sever a finger.

In the trap, they jostled like stones.
I topped the cooler brimful of ice
and seawater, morgue-cold.

My father fed them into the slush
with a sous-chef's precision.
I watched their sparring slow.

Haymakers blurred to lurches,
then quarter-inch twitches,
then nothing. They went under.

Drifting in the polar slurry
the crabs made a sinister clacking.
Their sleep was deep, deep.

Sometimes I'd reach in to stroke one—
a blue-black granite chassis
underlaid with a fidgetry of limbs.

When it came time to butcher them,
my father laid each on the jetty,
tenderly stroked the thorax

then drove his crabbing knife
clean through the brain.
He said it was humane—

but for a moment they'd come alive again,
legs unspringing their hinges,
pincers grappling at air.

In the neurological ward
I remember this
as I watch my father wake.

I won't come back, he said pre-op
but he did. He hallucinates,
lunges at things I can't see.

A sudden twist in the bedsheet—
he sits, beatific, and takes the invisible
delicately between two fingers

like a pinch of salt
or sheet of Belgian linen.
When I reach to receive it

his hand clamps on my wrist
and I am stunned by the strength
of his grip—like the claw

severed from the body
still grasping closed, like the mind
exposed under an oval of bone

to a shock of raw breeze—
for the first time, the last time
he wants to live.

Neurostimulator

The transhuman future
arrives for my father
as a matchbox purring in his chest—
battery pack biohacking
his brain, titanium ingot
shrink-wrapped in skin.

A wisp of silver cable
running up his spine is visible
only in silhouette
when he turns his neck—
subcutaneous ripple
threaded to his cortex.

After the surgery
his forehead buckles with a scar—
a runnel ringing his crown
like the trace of Roman fortifications
on a bald hillside, a ghost yarmulke.

Underneath, a confetti
of microelectrodes receives pulses
from his chest, urging
his neurons: connect.

But the man who always
adored machine logic
resents being programmed.
He blames the box

for each misjudged step,
his faltering, arrhythmic gait—
all signs of rebel code.

He only learns later
about the risks of malware—
his firewall is vulnerable,
any minute his microchip
could be hacked,
he could be made to moonwalk,
sent haywire, surveilled.

They say the server is secure
but there's no way to be sure.
My father's face unreadable
stone as he insists
his mind is his and his alone.

The Night Shift

Like hummingbirds attending
to injections of nectar

nurses squeak from room to room
in white sneakers. Buzzers

zip and sting like electric
whipbirds. My mother presses

David Attenborough to her ear—
his voice eases through the plastic

receiver. A caiman floats
in the Pantanal's scum green,

a crown of orange butterflies
sipping tears from its eye's skin. Salt

crystals sugaring each wingbeat.
Her chemotherapy drips. Night

cinches its tendrils around
blinking fluorescents—

light that will not die.
My mother drifts in and out

of a sleep that never
settles, but rises and dips

and rises. She's bone tired. The eye
of the caiman opens and closes—

slick membrane clinging
to never-ending saltlick. It's unclear

if it feels the infinitesimal weight lift
when each butterfly takes flight.

Maidenhair

It exploded from my mother's cutting—
combustible flare
skirting the green edge of morning,

a moat of unending motion
crowd-surfing the air.
Its invasion was incremental—

first a cluster, spade-cut
from my grandmother's garden
after the funeral, ferried home

in our canary-yellow Holden
and buried in a rubble of shadow
between fiddle-leaf and flax.

Then the creep—sprigs
patrolling the pavers,
a quick prickle of stems.

After rain, sudden detonation:
black bamboo stakes
flounced with shavings of lettuce,

jostling with jurassic spears
of birds-of-paradise,
that pterodactylic splay of flames.

Between breaths
you could hear each leaf
twitching. Cuttles and quills

in paisley formation,
undersides pimpled
with gooseflesh.

Today, twenty years late,
I find it in the garden, still
practising its one idea to exhaustion—

shivering leaflets
moving in anxious jubilation,
pockets of eternal thicket,

while I tipple on the edge
of the uncurling present,
watching my life harden into its one shape

the way my grandmother
smoothed her hair each morning
into a standing wave.

Vital Signs

Nurses flank my mother like bridesmaids
in lavender gowns and gloves.

One wheels a lavender trash-can
beside her bed—coded reliquary

for her toxic body.
Poison pulses above my mother's head,

a sluggish bladder
coffined in a violet sleeve,

a diaphanous chrysalis
too hazardous to touch.

The clipboard where nurses jot
vitals, urine and bloods

is the colour of the jacaranda tree
blossoming outside

because it is November, season of trampled
purple on the cricket field

behind the hospital where children
bat in match-day whites—

a roasting wind driving ash
and burnt grass into their lungs,

red leather cracking
like dry thunder on willow,

the air everywhere glazed with smoke
from distant fires making themselves known.

III

Instructions for a Lover

Bring me lemons and mint, a pitcher's fishbowl
loaded with ice and slices of cucumber,

a Tom Collins in a tumbler, the fizz of it.
Give me sulphur summer heat, tarry sidewalks,

a tired hydrant geysering over the street,
a plane ticket to the Virgin Islands or Madrid

and Saturday languor, bedsheets wicking away
sweat after sex, buy me a highball from a hotel bar

in another hemisphere, book me a room
at the Savoy or the Ritz, play me sweet low cello

or Carmen McRae, pour me a glass of Beaujolais,
give me an argument I can sink my teeth into all week,

learn how to dig in your heels, for god's sake,
slap me clean across the face with Riviera breeze,

and above all, take note of all the things I say—
pull me closer, push me away.

Epithalamium

Any wonder he tossed back Sazeracs and sidecars,
the one who always woke sullen
as the long blue light between buildings,
who slept with his back curled
like an accusation, who rocked
his weight onto his heels like an amateur
actor overdoing Stanley in *Streetcar*
when he hailed his cab in the morning.
Any wonder there were apologies
and bodega flowers wreathed with baby's breath,
any wonder there was another woman
I never met and then the wedding invitation,
no warning. He knew he was handsome—
his worst gift. In restaurants he ordered
without asking—steak tartare, dollop of yolk
glistening in raw meat. To love a narcissist
you have to believe, and reader, I did—
for a time, I loved him, I believed
in his cruelty and beauty—buds in silver
birch, sparrows scuffling
in the gravel by the basketball court
where I watched him play Sunday pick-up—
his brute musculature twisting
beneath his t-shirt, the springtime
itch of him—O, I believed as he shoved
and dodged his way up to dunk, I believed
as he spun that pebbled orange leather
in his fingertips like a cartographer
turning the first terrestrial globe,

its oceans gathered at the poles
like the curtains of a diorama,
its continents warped and stretched—
I believed the swish I heard
was the susurrus of reeds
on the bank of a blessed body of water,
I believed in his first principles and precepts—
and what I remember best
is how the ball slipped over the lip
then hung there a second—
a midair moon in the shredded net.

Classical Allegory

To hell with what you think of me.
I've started drinking martinis at three.
I wake, I walk, I write, I sleep.
I snooze the alarm. I doze. I read.
Sometimes I listen to Nina Simone
and pity you an inch. Not often.
Mostly I think about who'll be next
now you're gone. I stay out extravagantly late.
I buy myself a new coat, oysters, peonies.
I take long baths with a flute of champagne.
In bars, I sip whisky straight. I pet
stray cats on stoops. When it's hot
I laze around in French lingerie. Why not?
You've gone; the world hasn't stopped.

Affidavit

Fly me on a Lear jet to Antibes
      and lay me in state on a sunflower chaise.
Read me the rich list. I want to be chased
      with coconut oil and redacted
behind Jackie O shades. I've got equity
      in this Vieux Carré and a line
of credit from Bermuda to Biarritz—
      the deficit can wait.
Some weeks are only worth the whistle and list
      of superyachts in the wind,
so sing me their names:
      Nirvana, Eros, Zenith, Eclipse.
Heaven is an offshore haven
      where the dossier of my mistakes
is marked for immediate destruction
      and the grand jury's excused
and never seen or heard from again.
      My days are wide open and stacked
like Baccarat chips and there's nothing
      on my slate, so until the charges
against me are finally laid,
      register your complaint in writing
and address it care of Grand Cayman,
      and goddamn it, I'm so sick
of these surplus supermoons—
      if another one doesn't come round
this century it won't be too soon.

Parable of the Clubhouse

When it ended, he said I had never let him in—
as if I were a country club with a strict dress code
and he'd been waiting outside all those years
without his dinner jacket, staring in
at the gleaming plates of lobster thermidor,
scores of waiters in forest green blazers,
and the stout square shoulders of other men
who alternated tweed and seersucker over the seasons,
silver cloches ringing them in at dinner like bells—
so I said, maybe you're right, maybe that's how it is,
when you wanted a table I was always full,
when you want a table in the future I'll be full then too,
I'm booked out permanently, and no, you can't borrow
a coat, you have to bring your own, that's our policy.

Cipriani
—for E.

We were having dinner with a millionaire
        and drinking Russian Bellinis
when you said you were bored,

your red dress flaring out like a remedy
        in the clatter of crystal and china,
magnums of Pol Roger in gold tubs,

antipasti of octopus and bread,
        that beautiful heavy Italian bread
in perfect ovals on the side plates,

everything leavened, everything rising,
        your wrist holding the flute so evenly,
both of us waiting for the anecdote

about New Year's in Bahrain to end,
        the flat affectless fact of the £25,000 hotel,
waiting, waiting, and the waiters

bringing platefuls of thickly cut cake,
        moving like sharks between the tables,
their hands so sure, calling out

as the roulette wheel of the door poured in
        financiers and their exhaustingly
beautiful women, our Dover sole

and asparagus arriving on the pale
       flesh of a dish, oregano, lemon,
then you waspishly called them Eurotrash,

dismissed the whole affair—the stately tedium,
       the low-cut dresses, the high necks,
the projected dividends of our interest.

On Tiepolo's *Cleopatra*

Isn't this how we've always been, the men
leaning forward and the women lounging back
quick, mercurial, one arm extended
and one on the hip, as if to say is this your best,
you fool with your centurions and hounds,
your petty banquet, your fat explosions
of candied fruits on a platter, gleaming pewter,
this is your idea of wealth, is this all it takes
to woo you, poor rubes, there is a land beyond metaphor
there are luxuries beyond empire's comprehension—
and to prove the point, I'll swallow a pearl.

Ode to Cartier

I want to be decked and set—
smoke rolling from my *porte-cigarette*,

plush as a leopard's pelt,
decreed by royal warrant.

Knuckledust me—a bling
of cabochons like eggs—

a hatchery of bonbons
bulbous on every appendage.

O spangled, O sparkling—
drip me in onyx, pin me a wildcat

lumped with diamonds,
blunt club of the head

dewdropped in emerald, then clip
platinum lianas to my wrist.

Hunter, huntress—
there's life in me yet.

Fetch my tiger lorgnette,
snap tourmaline crocodiles at my neck,

pour me into the oval yawn
of a molten gold python,

then drag me to the greenest tips
of a coral tree, let me die in peace

with the silk of a jaguar's breath
huffing in my ear at dawn.

Alaska

It's late June in New York
the week of the Claremont triple homicide
and our bodies lie tranquil as chalk
in the white noise of my air-conditioning.
Last night they found three men
on this block in a gold Mercedes:
shot straight through the neck,
still buckled to their seats. Miles away
my father is disappearing, but for once I'm happy
listening to you talk in the dark.
You're telling me about Pasadena, the year
you got your licence. You were sixteen.
You spent the whole summer fishing
with your best friend. You'd take his dad's truck
to the canyon and drink, talk baseball,
see who could piss furthest in the river.
You hardly caught a thing, but that
wasn't the point. Buzzed on the drive back,
you'd almost clock a deer, swerve,
and watch it light off into redwoods.
Your voice is serious, you who have never
been serious about a single thing.
You're thinking about that place again
because this weekend your friend's father
drove that same truck to your fishing spot,
called 911 to tell them his wife's name
then shot himself in the parking lot:
no note, no nothing. The newspaper said
he was facing financial difficulties. *Facing*.

And in the huge silence we lie in
I think of Alaska, the late dog salmon
I saw struggling upstream in August, rotten red,
half-dead but still swimming.
The way they moved was like ice melting
and you could see everything in them was failing.
I turn to you to say I blame them, these fathers
who do not wait to see us grow up
or what we make of their tyrannical love
but you're silent, already sleeping,
and morning is coming on again, another morning.

The Proposal

He swore he understood it was over
then he flew to New York to propose.
First I knew was when he called me
from the arrivals hall. I could hear
announcements booming, the chatter
of passengers who had dozed beside him
as he thumbed the velvet capsule
of his fat half-carat secret,
I could hear families trundling luggage
and shrugging on coats around him,
I could see him standing with his duffel
in the centre, rock in a fast-moving river.
Soon he would be speeding towards me on Riverside—
his cheek pressed to winter glass
skin oiled by the long flight.
When he arrived, his face was from another life.
His voice was like a seventies sitcom—
suffocatingly nostalgic. I remember my dread
as we sat under Sarabeth's homely green awning.
I remember his tears falling, falling
when the waitress brought us a basket
of muffins—pumpkin, strawberry—
I remember the heat as I bit in, pure, searing.
I watched him eat his eggs. I leaned back
in the farmhouse chair. I hated him
for making me say it. No, I would not
marry him. No, I would never. After
we walked in the park. Sky the frostiest blue.
Cardinals like red bombs in bare limbs.

The reservoir frozen over, snow mounded on the verges.
You're so hard, he told me. He said it
like an indictment, as if presenting proof
of something I did not know—
but I already knew, and I did not rise
to object, because I praise whatever it is
in me that is stony and unbending,
I praise my hardness,
to it and it alone I say I do.

Night Flight

As my plane drops down in turbulence
I think of you and of Salt Lake City,
I think of ice stealing over the Great Lakes
and of Omaha and adamant plains.
I think of all the places
I have never been: Caracas,
La Paz, Kingston. I think of the way
our bodies puzzled together in that room
over pine woods where night deer
passed in the snow, their lonesome
inscrutable tracks sluicing
in the morning's melt, I think of
your eyes that are almost the colour
of mercury, of their unbearable weight,
I think of the plateau of your chest
rising, rising, and of your hand
resting on my thigh in the predawn light.
I think of how everything is defined
by distance: how close we were,
how far from steel mills in Pittsburgh
and those killing Chicago winds
and union towns near Detroit, Michigan
where loyalty is the only religion.
I think of the sound of your breathing,
which is the sound of fields
of blond Illinois wheat bent down,
I think of those silver silos
of harvest corn we saw in Schuylerville,
barns blazing in all that silence

as we drove through what we could
not think or say. There is no grace
in this kind of longing, there is only pain,
pain which I have always preferred
anyway—it is where I live,
and called love by any other name.

The Worst of It

As I combed it,
he sat cross-legged
in front of me,
bent over
like a penitent,
his head heavy
as intimacy.
An easy gesture,
like wind riffling
blue dunegrass
in tidal weather.
Salt and pepper
at the temples,
or more accurately
silver, perilous
and stellar.
A wave in it,
long from lack
of cutting.
How can I go back
to knowing nothing,
knowing this?

Mansions

When I think of you, I think of mansions—
those white porches we drove past in Schuylerville,
Adirondack chairs mounded with snow,
Grecian columns on Saratoga's racing homes,
fairy lights strung from the eaves like icicles
knife-bright in spring, and of that one house on Union
with uterine ovals of flowers for Easter,
rose and yellow, scalloped garlands on the gates.
I think of the rooms inside those mansions,
the hushed cold floors, marble quarried
in Danby by men whose hands are like stone,
smooth and cool, men who nurse long beers
and live outside town. I think of the women
who love them, those men who made these mansions,
and of the space inside them for love,
the high-arched ceilings of it, the echoing corridors
lit by Tiffany glass, the milk-and-white swirl
of leadlight windows in harlequin patterning,
all those diamonds breathing in light.

Blue Quandong

Nights here are long—
starlight frays the palms,

sky a black sarong
shaken out to dry.

I hear emerald doves
in the calabash.

I see the thousand flowers
of the cannonball tree.

I remember pepper leaf,
the singe of torch ginger—

think of you on the equator
from these cooling tropics.

I miss you—
a line I would never write.

Grief is rebetiko
heard through an open window

as the quandong
fruits at dusk—

wild basilica
distilling its sugars

into flying fox nectar,
rounding its midnight planets

of Marrakesh indigo,
an orrery of blue moons.

Serious Moonlight

Sleepless in a hotel room over Lipari
I lose my breathing
in your chest's slow piston—

a single wooden craft
sculling at midnight
towards some blind island.

We are the rower and the rowed
in Böcklin. I taste resin
from black cypress,

tincture of rockrose, bassia.
You are lost in the oarwork
of your lungs, loose arcs

that never come full circle.
The moon is not enough for us.
There is some other light

basting my skin: white, funereal.
I breathe in—my coffin
glides soundless behind me.

I breathe out—basalt
sea stacks swim
into sight, all that is mortal

by my side. I see a water gate—
a chink in the stone.
Vertigo, a dazzled tempo.

And I know wherever I am going—
Pontikonisi, Strombolicchio—
I will go alone.

IV

Driving Through Drystone Country

Paddocks hinge open in the mind—
vast watercolour pans
wetted with mizzling rain.

A single-carriage road
cuts through the valley
in oxbow arcs, stout stone walls

hemming either side,
clear as the divide
between thought and belief.

Dreadlocked sheep
marked for slaughter
with punk spray-paint

roam the fog grass,
pagan gods of lichen and moss
chewing over the long view

of kinking macadam.
Range Rovers kick up
a spittle of gravel round the bends.

Bronze field barns
slope in local vernacular—
sandstone cubed with a level eye,

quoins of gritstone
bracketing each corner.
Slovenly roofs pitch

over hay store and cow stall—
industry of the particular—
and everywhere the regular metre

of drystone walls,
arrowheads of shale
fitted with flagstone precision.

Monuments to nothing
but labour and time.
Plein-air altars for rain and wind.

Gin & Tonic at the Rock Hotel

Tonight Morocco's mountain disappears
into rafts of lilac mist. I raise a cut-glass
tumbler on the balcony—quinine swims
melancholy on the tongue. Under Art Deco arches
red and pink geraniums are bolted
to the wall in blue pots, blunt assertions
of beauty. Stars like rivets over rusted gun batteries.
Across the strait, Algeciras's lights wink in code.
Here civility and acrimony sway cheek to cheek—
barbary apes swing and call in the gardens
under the shadow of the cable car
that shudders up the Rock,
and old stands of cacti branch to the sky.
In the lobby bar, expats bicker about Brexit
and divorcees flirt with Spanish waiters.
A guest complains to the girl at reception
because his butter came in a wrapped pat.
It's vulgar, he says. Tomorrow the mountain
may or may not reappear
and I will hear yellow-legged gulls
screaming in the thermals as I wake.

Lago Nicaraguense

Like tourist talk at the Quay
the Carnival is rum and superficial cheer.
Americans with camcorders stand back
to let the flamenco dancers pass—
local girls hyacinthed like beauty queens,
their skirts bright as Florida wallpaper—
and Germans pick through rattan baskets
for Chiclets and Elephant cigarettes.
The local men stand back and smoke.
I know one of them, an old Cuban
who plays saxophone at the steakhouses with his son.
He nods at me as I pass.
He is drunk but mostly happy,
hates Castro, will never go home.
The women's bangles are colourblocked Kodachrome.
Their red and white skirts pinwheel
faster and faster in the afternoon sun
as the local priest picks through for offerings.
Even his cassock tassels seem gaudy
though across the street is shanty poverty
where candy-coloured bars and colonial yellow
give way to dirt road and tarp.
Violeta stares from her pedestal in the Parque.
I follow the procession to the lake
where papier-mâché skeletons rise overhead
and a costumed girl wades shoeless at the water's edge,
looking out to Concepción.
The islands drift off under the volcano's shadow
and the day pours out like Flor de Caña,
blocks of ice in a thick blue glass.

Quetzalcoatl
—*for Vera Pavlova*

On the bus to Teotihuacan, we turn
a new god's name on our tongue

like a charm, jagging past
cinderblocked hills

chocked over the motorway,
grey pixels stacked so high they merge

with the smoked white Mexican sky—
then a guitar player in the aisle

begins a song whose only familiar
word is *corazón*, and we move on, billboards

graffitied *Narco Estado* scream by,
and I think of the jostling in the plaza

last night during the Ayotzinapa strike,
candlelight salving poster faces

of the missing, and wonder
whether there is a god

who bothers to bless those who travel
on buses, not only those who scale

blunt steep steps of pyramids
where the world bends to an untenable angle

as if to say, kneel, human,
your heart isn't enough—

give me your life.

Sketches from the Nile

I.

You tilt water to your lip—
a day light as wicker.

By the river, bulrushes bow
into sailboat blue, lace-necked

egrets fossick and pick,
and the elements rearrange

a goliath heron's skull to mud.
On the embankment

a crouching child scratches
his name into a temple wall.

II.

Ultramarine, lapis lazuli—
today it seems possible to boil

queens to bone and paint,
unlike our childhood saints

whose vigils never cease,
whose faces do not age.

Feluccas rock in afternoon sun,
yellow licks of light

hammer the Nile to scale.
In a valley near Thebes, antique heads

suffocate in starless catacombs,
linen figure-eighting the face,

jewel blue basting the eyelids,
the last cold smears of sky.

III.

A sprint of sandpipers
on mudflats, a low hammock.

Thought flakes away.
History is a headless dog

on the road to Karnak
where a tribe of sparrows

excavate the bones
of old sparrows, digging

in the mortar for a home.
Buried in the stucco there

you might find a blue splinter,
a figure for a mortal skull.

Meditation on Risk in New Hampshire

Running down tracks of Colorado blue spruce
to the trailhead, I hit the end of the ploughed path
and head into new snow—*brak da bruid*,
they say in Shetland, the first foot
after snowfall—and as my feet compact
powder I think of the conversation
I had last night with the Mexican filmmaker
who grew up with a pet jaguar in Sinaloa—
a gift from her father, a man she called
a *character*—and how she loved that cat,
how she used to sit with it, even after
it tore apart her brother's beagle and ate it.
Manuelito, the jaguar's name was—Manuelito
who lived in the garden of the family's motel
deep in drug country, where Saturday night their bar
was full of cartel kingpins and local police,
a place where nobody thought anything about giving
a girl a pet jaguar who could crunch
through her skull, whose key method of killing
is by piercing the brain itself—
and I ask myself why the body courts
proximity to what can kill it, the surfer
paddling into Great White territory off Rottnest,
the base-jumper stepping into a white triangle of air,
the man who corresponds on the internet
with a German fetishist who writes of nothing
but how he would butcher and eat him.
In Alaska, my friend and I turned the corner
on a trail of currant and bayberry

and walked into a standing grizzly. I remember
how it reared to full height to see what we were,
the mason's block of its jaw,
how it lumbered after us down the slope
to the braided river—clear water, grey stones cutting
through foothills—then gorged on soapberries,
holding our lives hostage for minutes. I could hear
panic in the throat of my friend, her shallow breaths—
but what I remember best is not terror
but the sound of water from the wild creekbed,
pine, flowering balsam, evergreen.

Upon Viewing a Still Life by Chardin and Thinking of the Marathon Bombing in Boston

Begin with the hock of a leg, brisk
   whisk of flight, the flex, the weft
that batters over lake, stutters into sky
     and gives the mallard life
       or what we think of as life, which is movement—

frieze of a duck's leg pointed to the ceiling, red flare,
   and below, like a snagged handkerchief
the body droops, forever hurtling
     towards the mannered Mediterranean
       accoutrements: lemon, olives, brown loaf of pâté—

forever hurtling, and think, you have only one morning
   in which to imagine this—that is,
many possible lives
     but one death only,
       which we will not admit is the only constancy,

one death, one trajectory—it is so difficult
   to imagine, driving out of Springfield, Massachusetts
in a clotted summer morning,
     so difficult to convince ourselves
       these are our bodies, these are our corpses.

In the painting by Chardin we are in the scullery,
    the piece of linen is too-blanched, too-hushed,
and the beautiful victim: cloud-white, cloud-grey
        the world winnowing into its face, its body
            dangling over Capri lemon, fresh air, eighteenth century

light imbuing everything with gravitas—be still,
    be still, death is forever but if you are still
you will master it, you too will
        be beautiful—then in the radio chatter
            suddenly they are talking about the marathon

in Boston and how they will kill him, the Kyrgyzstani boy
    with the backwards cap who hefted
death in his athletic bag, the one
        with a dreamer's face like a Titian who blew
            apart all those legs, those arms, those bodies

mashing in the unexpected moment—tragedy
    arriving instead of triumph—but it does that,
masked, enters unannounced—and often in the canvas
        we mistake it for beauty, completion masquerading
            as perfection, death, the finished artefact—

so dearly the state wants to kill him—
    lustre of porcelain and sheen of fat—
as they talk about importing the dose, how they will do it
        I see that death is an embellishment, that what
            is important is the ceremony, the arrangement,

as in the painting—the dead are so obliging, so still—
    they let everyone in,
crush of linen, gleam of glass, and above,
        the game suspended perpetually, as if there is
          any artful way to hang a living thing.

Monopoli

Tonight I dreamt again of Monopoli—
its red and blue boats smacking
in the harbour,
its dusty white stones.

I dreamt of Monopoli's fishermen
hauling white anchovies and sardines,
livid squid in morning light,
blue nets beaded with salt.

I dreamt of the *lungomare*
crusted with detritus
from Europe's shipping lanes—bottles,
rope, buoys pitted with barnacles.

There was a square there
where I drank wine
with hard olive biscuits
twisted like crowns.

Down by the port, after, I saw
a pair of lovers
in the filleting air
watching wave after wave after wave.

On Worthing Beach

Night, I walk a coastline divided
into shingle bays—

each racketing its shallow tray
of pebbles like shrapnel.

Rollers gutter and dump
in Atlantic swell—

wind cuts through to my skull.
Hauled up on the rocks,

the empty hulls
of beached trawlers glitter

under a phosphorous moon.
I climb into one—

its ragged net
sections the sky

into frayed quadrants,
maps the zirconia stars.

Spread on the deck
black bream scales

are lustrous
as molten glass

in the moonlight.
Offshore, shoals of pilchards

glint like silver tailings
in the chalk reefs—

each retaining a buffer
of space around it,

a small assertion of selfhood.
My own life is dividing—

the life I have already lived
gaining on the years left—

but tonight I am free
to run to the pier's end—

take a sudden weightless dive,
weathered pilings

rising like headstones
around me in the surf,

groynes slanting into the longshore drift.
I would do it for the cold,

the hallowed and hallowing cold—
perforate the water's surface,

skin of cellophane wrinkling
over liquid agate.

I do not jump.
I skulk the empty pavilion—

the amphitheatre's shell
cluttered with equipment

from summer rides:
spinning teacups, the mallet

from a high striker
propped against a pillar.

There is a grief
that rides alongside me—

cigarette
that will not extinguish

burning its bitumen
at the back of the throat.

An oily capsule of light
coats the fish and chip shop—

the door a rectangle
into the familiar

ghost of my father
who is everywhere and nowhere now

still sitting at a counter somewhere
waiting for his cod to come.

A Handful of Oranges

Rinds of shadow
tossed
in the white courtyards
of Andalusia.

*

Midday, men thrash
overloaded lemon trees
with poles
in the Alcázar's gardens:
thudding bombardment,
hail of acid.

*

La Giralda's bells ring
like sirens
over the city's holy domes—
dimpled grenades
curdling
their bitter honey.

*

All day the rustling grove
builds its wild frescoes.
Beyond the gate,
an overflowing blue skip

mounded
with harvest moons.

*

Boiled, sour oranges
sputter to candied marmalade—
but only in English kitchens.

*

A murmur of tourists
cupped
in a church's ceiling.
Talk fills a space—
silence rounds it.

*

After days of Seville's circle mosaics
and gold duomos
packed with sun
I am stunned
by the sudden sweetness
of chopped orange wood
by the fireplace.

Forgive me—
I burned it.

Great North Road

At the mountain's mouth
I wait for admission
to the Great North Road.

Pearls of condensation hang
from the clagged roof
like stop-motion rain.

My hardhat's beacon
lights up a wall of black-
and-white photographs,

a soldier who looks like me
then doesn't again.
It's in the eyes. Three years

my grandfather lived
inside this mountainhead
nosing molewards in the dark,

geligniting boltholes,
hammer-drilling clearances
for bunkers and roads.

A puff of seaspray
ghosts my neck—I turn
to a blowhole in the stone.

The tunnel curves ahead—
bone marrow offcut,
artery of skinned limestone

that could stretch east
to Bahía Dorada
if ironed straight

but instead kinks
and burrows inwards,
pinch of frazzled nerves.

Ahead, the path branches
into half-pipes of Nissen huts
where nurses staunched

butchered tendons
of infantrymen
hazed with morphine—

ersatz windows fitted
beside each bed
to keep them on the beam.

The walls are nicked
by diamond drills,
scratching of graffiti.

I hunt for my grandfather's initials,
for his three claustrophobic years
of sunless labour.

Nothing. A submarine net coils
by the wall, metal nautilus.
Shifts of juddering excavation

rattled by the sorties
of Italian Piaggios, frogmen,
German limpet mines—

only a few portholes
cutting to a flickering view
of skewering searchlights.

I see him sleeping
in a hurricane lamp's
orange lozenge

before he climbs out
of the mountain to sketch
the wind-scoured slope,

back wrecked from drilling,
his work not building
but emptying, quarrying

like a shipworm
eating through limestone,
his paintings always

oriented away and not
towards the Rock—
wash of early evening

cloud building over Ceuta,
date palms in Rosia Bay,
a flotilla of warships

trailing swerves
of gasoline in the strait,
rain over the tip of Africa,

the whole narrowing world
coming and going
in the steel-backed light.

Mediterranean Steps

Worn loaves of limestone
piled in a lumbering tetris
climb with breath-snatching depth
past leathery leaves of wild olive
sea lavender and candytuft,
bluest shadows of carob trees.
I stop on an outcrop.
I want but cannot find
the precise perspective
of my grandfather's painting
made here in 1943—
dizzying upwards view
of the angular peak, deep
stairs overgrown by giant
gold tassels of Tangiers fennel.
I crane my neck at each rickracking
turn, crouch to find his perch.
An out-of-season Egyptian vulture
tilts in the breeze. Wild jasmine
simmers. This place
is mine and not mine—
its thickets of maquis
that gripped the wall
of my childhood bedroom
familiar yet wirier,
the sandblasting wind
more violent, the terror
of the drop impossible
to anticipate from a watercolour—

still I love knowing nobody
is here but me, the steps empty
as they are in his painting,
the vantage point inscrutable,
the self implied but illegible
among the nettles and stone pines.

In My Father's Country

I.   The Burr

It is guesswork, this slattern backcountry
I climb in darkness:

ice shirring gunmetal moors,
each hillock and rise

a cairn of tortoise stones,
slate in skid and trip steps.

I have come hunting you
where the cottage moon roosts,

I have scouted
the cold declensions of the stars

for your lagered vowels, the slough
and guff of pub talk and grift,

but all I have is a map of burrs,
places you have clung, the briar catch,

the pinch of cobbler's peg at each
clench of the years, the heart's geography

stymied by the fuse-bright blur
of Yorkshire's border lights,

and I do not know my way.
There is no evidence of the pear trees

you shinned, that hedgerow berried
with your scarred blood,

no ruins of the lime mortar
and granite house where you grew,

no symbology of rune and henge
I can read here in the dark.

Mist scuttles the barns,
the world tipples into fog,

black exhalations of woodsmoke
from workers' chimneys purl out.

Still, I look in every skirled pane
for proof of you, a lilt, a laugh,

a coat on a hook holding
the shape of an arm.

II.   *Your Dying*

Late, late, late, late, late.
You are late in your dying.

You, who always scarfed
your food before all,

a public school habit
forged in the war

where marrow was swopped
for jam, mutton for lamb;

you who finished first, dux, swot;
you who pathologically topped:

you are late. I can forgive
you your dying but not this

insistence. You always said
you'd go swift. I hate

that you've stayed. You took
your mind first, *bon mots*,

gallows wit, but still
your body persists. Your dying

has taken the better part
of two decades, as if,

handed this one last task,
you have resolved

to do it exhaustively—
methodical, a pedant above all—

but how can I deny you your time?
It's your curtain call, your fall,

and though you always loved
baroque efficiencies, in the end

you're less Bartók than Prokofiev,
a heavy touch, bombast and squall.

III.   The Hex

Your mother loved the bottle
but you were jovial, semi-teetotal,

somehow immune from the streak
of drink running matrilineally—

a swig, a swoon, the room awash
in a flush of swinging light—

that giddy rotten freedom
you eschewed for life.

Painful, then, that the hex
found you in another way:

sober syllables uttered drunk,
the slur, the sliding vowels,

the creeping lisp of Parkinson's.
Indignities compound. Language

sluices away from you, bolts
like a gelding from the box.

In fright you find yourself half-cut
without a sip, your throat

uncooperative, over-oiled,
the words scrambling in a rush,

a stutter, a cable in garbled Morse
not even you can decode.

IV.   Long Division

Each car ride with you was a test—
so sorely you wanted

a mathematician. You got
a daughter instead: wilful, uninterested

in inverse relations. We drove
Bournemouth to Land's End,

each groyne and harbour wall
pebbled with unnavigable stone

as you drily taught, blue anorak
zippered to the neck. I knew

how to disappoint, feigned boredom.
Pigheaded, I picked over tchotchkes

in seaside shops, chucked gulls
sodden chips, ignored your puzzles.

When you gave me equations
I turned to the window in a snit—

class dismissed. My stupidity served me
poorly; adult, I can barely add.

But sometimes when lecturing
a subdued hall, I hear your ghost,

or its confident hectoring gist:
that is to that as this is to this.

V. *Antipodes*

Delighted by tomcats and squirrels,
kinder in general to animals,

you confused with your tenderness.
Mostly you were shy,

shy with your daughter, your wife.
As though a too-loud word,

a shout might blow away
your precarious new life.

I was always unclear
about the lure of your long exile

to the antipodes, though as an adult,
I understand the urge to clear

house, start again—I do it
almost every year.

If you felt disdain
it was rarely on display,

still, your learning was lost
on your new continent: dull friends

you incited futilely to read
The Late George Apley,

guffawing in-laws baffled
by your banter at Christmas lunch,

your annual homilies on Churchill's
History of the English-Speaking Peoples

growing quietly strident
over lukewarm prawns.

VI.   *Anti-Gravity*

For science, you took me to the beach
to test the weight of sand. I scooped and scraped

three grades: shelly stuff, squeak quartz,
volcanic black, winnowed and watered

between my hands. You looked on,
watched the dark surge in my palms,

a cradle I could not keep,
expounded something about physics

though it did not stick. Terminally
bored, I was deaf to your brilliance.

Next year we tried my idea,
hammered a pendulum

from our cat's post, revisited gravity.
I watched the lead sinker

swing toward me, grasped it,
let it go. You were so

patient as I reeled through
bunkum theories, lobbed

leading questions
to turn me round. Finally

I understood what made
things fall. Now, when you

ramble and loop
in the roil of your mind,

I see that line swing out—
nothing can bring it down.

VII.   *A Brief History of the British Raj*

I was never good at being public.
Neither were you.

Clammily private, in your better mind
you kept schtum about family.

Unknown, unseen, they were a gap
where I alchemised: the sooty face

of my grandfather's *Self-Portrait in Oil*,
hawkish glowering brows

so like my own, his watercolours
of Algeciras posted home

to Harrogate, sketches of downed
bridges in wartime France

where he was bombed from the sky
and hurtled you to solitude

in that house with your mother's stockpile
of rum—all fodder. They were never quite real.

In your decline, though, you're expansive,
fluent in the unverifiable.

Like the news you delivered last week
that half the family was British Raj—

my grandfather born in India,
boarded at the Bishop Cotton School,

my great-uncle the Postmaster General
of Bihar Orissa. Colonial anxieties

converge in my head, a tangle
of half-missed steps. And while

the names and dates are plausible,
your true origins are lost for good:

Worthing, Leeds or Bangladesh, all
unpronounceable and obscure as ash.

VIII.   *Brain Surgery*

As I snailed around the Vatican's
overblown putti skies

in the southern hemisphere
they were opening your brain.

Sawing off a neat cup of bone
then lifting it like a doffed cap,

probing the wet squelch for a spark,
electrodes basted to your temples

in a mimicry of electroshock—
bite down, bite down, soon

the lights will be out. Mid-anaesthetic,
though, they woke you up again,

made you lift an arm,
then a leg, squirrel your fingers

into fists, like a pet they were taking
through its paces. You didn't resist.

Like swimming, you said—swimming,
with a rod in your head.

IX.   *The Tremor*

We knew before the doctor did.
Your hand crabbing, its fits and starts

like a fieldmouse in scrabble panic,
the scribble of a cardiogram

drawn on air. Every gesture was loose.
Your motions were approximate,

missing the mark. There was nothing
to say, nothing still—

you were irate with your diagnosis.
The house quaked

under your powderkeg fuse. For weeks
you only addressed the cat,

sought its cool, contained ministry.
The anger didn't abate. You snapped,

jackal-mad, at the slightest
error. I learnt to stay away,

avoid asking, tiptoe across
faultlines I had no seismograph

to measure. It is years, but
the tremor still buckles and shakes.

X. *Indirect Address*

We've said our goodbyes—
you're elsewhere now.

Here, but nowhere really.
We only talk in poetry.

I'm not sure when
I last saw the you I knew—

whenever it was
I didn't make note of the date.

No fear. We were always bad
at ceremony—the cake uncut,

the gifts faintly embarrassing.
At times I glimpse

the iceberg tip
of your subterranean mind

but you're away mostly
and so am I. I'm sorry

we don't speak more often—
my syntax is broken.

Falsely cheery or stern,
I don't know how to address you,

how to be your parent.
I wish you could teach me

to be patient
but you've jumped the gun,

fastest off the mark
in the quickest sprint of all.

XI.   Winter, Worthing

You spent your war years
on Worthing's shingled seafront—

the beach blockaded with slabbed concrete
and wire to rout the Krauts.

Churchill said *they won't come by sea*,
but you lived in imminence

at the outbreak, sleeping
huddled in the front garden

before the Morrison Shelter arrived,
that suffocating quarter inch

of steel wrapped like a blanket
around your childhood.

Your mother paid peppercorn rent
for a house where you hardly slept

then you were exiled to board at twelve
when her boozing revved,

your father dead, your country
on ration. Now the shore

is a tip of crockery shale, soft glassfuls
rubbing it smooth, each heaving

wave stubbing out, beginning again.
Cheap trinket shops dot the front.

At night the lights spot on
like lanterns in rolling spray,

quaint font rocks and swings
on the gastropub. My whisky sears

and cracks its ice—the sting, the saw
of true north. Then I think of you

sleeping on your frozen front lawn.
And I cannot get warm.

Notes to the Poems

The book's epigraph is taken from 'Eros' by H.D. from *H.D. Selected Poems*, ed. Louis L. Martz, (New Directions, 1988), p. 33.

'Empires of Mind' takes its title from a speech Winston Churchill gave when being conferred with an honorary degree at Harvard in 1943, in which he said, 'The empires of the future are the empires of the mind.'

'Terminal Lucidity': Terminal lucidity is a deathbed phenomenon whereby those suffering from cognitive decline or psychiatric disorders regain their senses or memories in the hours or days preceding death.

'Pikes Peak': Pikes Peak is a fourteener mountain—rising more than 14,000 feet above sea level—located in Pike National Forest, Colorado; it is the highest summit of the Colorado Front Range of the Rocky Mountains.

'Substantia Nigra': Impairment of neurons in the midbrain's substantia nigra, along with the presence of Lewy bodies, causes a loss of dopamine that produces the motor symptoms of Parkinson's disease.

'Tijuana': El Santuario de Chimayó in New Mexico is a Catholic church famed for the reputedly miraculous powers of its holy dirt, known as *tierra bendita*. Pilgrims eat the dirt or rub it on their bodies; many leave their walking sticks, crutches and other aids in the church as evidence of the dirt's purportedly curative powers.

'Neurostimulator': This poem recounts the implantation of a Deep Brain Stimulator device.

'Serious Moonlight': This poem refers to the painting *Isle of the Dead* (*Die Toteninsel*) (May 1880) by Arnold Böcklin.

'Upon Viewing a Still Life by Chardin and Thinking of the Marathon Bombing in Boston' responds to the painting *Duck Hanging by One Leg, Pâté, Bowl and Jar of Olives* (1764) by Jean-Baptiste-Siméon Chardin.

'Great North Road': The Great North Road is the largest of a series of tunnels built during World War II inside the Rock of Gibraltar, as part of a massive expansion of a network of tunnels initially established during the Great Siege. At the height of the war, the Rock of Gibraltar housed an entire garrison of 16,000 troops and a bomb-proof city inside it, including a hospital, barracks, a generating station, a vehicle repair workshop and a water desalination plant. My grandfather, Bertram Batt—an architect and artist—was stationed as a Royal Engineer in Gibraltar during his service, and painted the landscape there extensively before his death in 1945.

Acknowledgements

Poems in this collection appeared in *The New Yorker*, *Poetry*, *Kenyon Review*, *Arc Poetry Magazine*, *The Monthly*, *The Australian*, *The Weekend Australian*, *Meanjin*, *HEAT*, *Australian Book Review*, *Westerly*, *The Red Room Company*, *Griffith Review*, *Reading the Landscape* (UQP), *Contemporary Australian Feminist Poetry* (Hunter) and the University of Canberra Vice Chancellor's Poetry Prize anthologies. My thanks to the editors of these publications. I am also grateful to Bronwyn Lea, Maria Takolander and Kevin Young for their readings of various poems.

I sincerely thank the Sidney Myer Foundation for the sustained support of a Sidney Myer Creative Fellowship; the Australia Council for the Arts, which supported the writing of these poems; and to Yaddo and MacDowell, where a number of these poems were written. I also thank the Fondation Heinrich Maria & Jane Ledig-Rowohlt for a Lavigny Fellowship at the Château de Lavigny, Switzerland.

This book is dedicated to my late father, Dr Anthony Bertram Holland-Batt (1937–2020), whose brilliance and kindness were larger than life, and are now larger than death.